KU-637-020

King Midas

Contents

Chapter 1	The Love of Gold	4
Chapter 2	Dionysus	7
Chapter 3	The Wish	12
Chapter 4	The Golden Touch	16
Chapter 5	A Blessing or a Curse?	22

Chapter 1

The Love of Gold

King Midas was the richest king in Anatolia. He lived in a magnificent palace and had everything that a king could ask for. Servants brought him the tastiest food to eat and the finest wine to drink. They tended the gardens where colourful roses bloomed.

Every evening, Midas would walk in the gardens with his daughter, Zoe.

"See how beautiful these flowers are," said Midas, pointing out a pink rose. "They are almost as beautiful as you."

King Midas

by Damian Harvey and Sonya Abby Soekarno

FRANKLIN WATTS

Zoe stopped to smell the rose. "And they smell just as beautiful as they look," she said.

Midas gently held up another rose. "But this one is surely the most beautiful of all," he said. "As bright and golden as the sun itself."

Zoe smiled sadly as her father admired the golden rose, because there was one thing she knew for sure. Her father loved many things, but there was one thing he loved above everything else – gold.

Every room in the palace contained gold. Golden statues stood in the hallways. Midas poured his wine from a golden jug and drank it from golden goblets. Servants laid his food on golden plates and brought it to him on fine golden trays.

His clothes were decorated with delicate golden stitches. Rings shone on his fingers and chains criss-crossed his chest.

Every day, Midas would sit in his vast treasure room to count his gold coins. Whenever Zoe couldn't find her father, she knew that was where he would be. But no matter how much gold Midas had, he always wanted more.

Chapter 2

Dionysus

Now, Dionysus, the son of the Greek God Zeus, was passing through King Midas's land, with his old friend and teacher, Silenus, and their companions. Zeus was the king of all the gods and so everywhere Dionysus went, he and his friends were entertained with the finest food and drink. They spent the day with Midas, drinking and eating, before finally going on their way.

The next morning, a servant woke Midas up.

"Sire," cried the servant. "We found this old man

asleep in your gardens. What shall we do with him?"

Midas sat up in bed and looked at the old man.

He saw the ropes around the old man's wrists

where the servants had tied him up.

Then he looked at the old man's face.

"You fools!" he cried. "This is Silenus. He was with

us yesterday at the palace. Untie him at once!"

The ropes fell away and Silenus rubbed his wrists.

"Do not be angry with your servants, Sire," he said.
"They were right to act as they did. Last night,
Dionysus and the others went off ahead of me.
I sat down for a rest and I must have fallen asleep.
When I awoke, your servants were tying me up."

Now, King Midas knew how powerful Dionysus was.
After all, his father was the king of the gods. What
would he do if he found out that Silenus had been
treated like this? Then Midas had an idea. "Please
stay here as my guest," he said, smiling at Silenus.
"Then, when you feel better, I will help you find
Dionysus."

Silenus happily agreed. For the next ten days,
he stayed as an honoured guest in the palace.

On the eleventh day, they set off to search for Dionysus and his companions. At last, Midas found them resting in the forest. Dionysus was delighted to see his old friend again. "I thought you had got lost," he laughed.

"Not at all," Silenus replied. "I have been a guest in Midas's palace. He has looked after me well."

"Thank you, King Midas," said Dionysus. "Not everyone treats my friend so kindly. As a reward, I grant you one wish. You may wish for whatever your heart desires. But think hard ... you have one wish, and one wish only."

Midas thought for a moment and then a smile slowly spread across his face.

Chapter 3

The Wish

"Gold!" he whispered, his eyes lighting up.

"But why?" Dionysus said, puzzled. "You already have more gold than anyone. Why would you want more when you can have anything else in the world?"

"But I do want more," said Midas, eagerly. "I want everything I touch to turn to gold."

"No! I will not grant this foolish wish," said Dionysus. "It is a wish that will bring you only sorrow."

"But think how beautiful the world would be if everything was gold," said Midas.

"No!" Dionysus repeated. "You must think of something else. Remember, you may wish for anything you like."

"Then I wish for gold," said Midas stubbornly. "I wish that everything I touch shall turn to gold."

Dionysus shook his head sadly, but there was nothing he could do. He had offered a wish and now he had to grant it.

"So be it," he said.

"From this moment on, everything you touch will turn to gold."

As Dionysus and his companions walked away,
King Midas felt a strange tingling feeling washing
over him like a wave. When the feeling passed,
Midas looked at his reflection in a pool of water.

"I don't look different," he said, frowning.
He reached out and touched a small twig.
There was a faint crackling sound in the air and
the twig turned to gold. Midas touched a small
stone. That too turned to gold.

Midas took the twig and
the golden stone and
examined them. "Gold,"
he marvelled.
"I've turned them
into gold."

Throwing them down, Midas reached out to an oak tree. He watched in wonder as, from the point where his hand touched, gold spread up the trunk until every branch and every leaf had been transformed.

"Gold!" Midas cried, stepping back to admire the tree. "And it's all mine!"

Midas walked thoughtfully back to the palace. "I don't want to share my gift with anyone," he said to himself. "I will keep every piece of gold for myself."

Chapter 4

The Golden Touch

As soon as King Midas reached his beloved
gardens, he touched a bright red rose. As it
turned to gold, Midas clapped his hands with joy.
He touched a pink rose and a white rose ...
and watched them all turn to gold.
"Even more beautiful than before," he declared.

He bent down to touch the grass and watched
with delight as it changed from lush green
to shining gold. It looked like a vast golden carpet
being unrolled before him. "The perfect thing
for a king to walk on," laughed Midas.

The king walked through the gardens touching plants and flowers. He smiled as each one was transformed. Ahead of him, Midas spotted Costa, the old man who tended the gardens.

"Look how beautiful the garden is today, Costa," he said. "Even more beautiful than yesterday." Costa turned round as the king approached. When he saw the golden roses, he looked shocked.

"Oh, my king, what have you done?" he cried.
"Watch," said Midas, reaching out to touch
the flowers that Costa was tending.

As the flowers turned to gold, the old gardener
let out a gasp. King Midas laughed at the look
on Costa's face, and gave him a friendly pat
on the shoulder. "Look, they're beautiful,"
said Midas, but the gardener didn't hear him –
he had turned to gold.

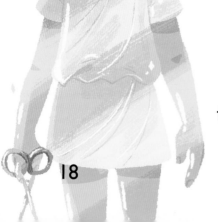

For a moment, King Midas
was taken aback, but then he
laughed. "What could be more
perfect than a golden gardener
for a golden garden?"

As King Midas went into his palace, he had never felt so happy. Dionysus had been wrong about his wish ... it wasn't foolish at all. It was something to celebrate.

After turning the tables, chairs and carpets to gold, Midas called his servants. "Bring a feast," he announced. "A feast to celebrate my wonderful gift. And flowers," he added. "Freshly cut flowers so that I can breathe in their beautiful fragrance."

While his servants prepared the feast, Midas went
to put on clean clothes. But every time he was
handed a new robe, it turned to gold.

"This won't do," said Midas. "Get me that one,"
he said, pushing his servant towards the cupboard.

Too late, Midas realised what he had done as
the servant turned to gold. Midas frowned, and
then shrugged.

"Oh well, who needs fresh clothes," he said
to the golden servant. "All I need is gold."

As Midas went back to the hall, a servant carrying a jug of wine tripped on a golden rug. Midas reached out to help him but no sooner had he caught the man's arm than he was turned to gold. Midas laughed as the servant and the jug of wine spilling into the air both became frozen in shining gold.

Chapter 5

A Blessing or a Curse?

Sitting on his throne, Midas reached for one of the freshly cut roses. As he lifted it, it turned to gold. Instead of the beautiful fragrance, all he could smell was metal.

Midas began to feel a little sad. "From now on," he realised, "I will have to smell the roses without touching them."

Without thinking, Midas reached for a bunch of delicious grapes. Before he'd even lifted them from their bowl, they were transformed into gold. "No!" cried Midas, suddenly feeling worried.

"This can't be right. Surely Dionysus realised I would need to be able to eat and drink."

One of the servants stepped forward. "I can help, my lord. Let me feed you," he said, and held out a grape. But as soon as the grape touched Midas's lips, both it and the servant turned to gold.

Midas cried out in anger, and grabbed his golden wine goblet. As it was already gold, there was nothing to transform. The king looked down at the wine in his goblet. Then he lifted it up and poured some into his mouth.

With a scream of rage and fear, Midas spat a mouthful of gold on to the floor. He grabbed hungrily at the food before him but it all turned to gold. "What am I to do?" he sobbed. "I shall starve!"

"What is it, Father?"

Midas turned to see his daughter, Zoe, reaching out for him.

"No!" he cried. "Don't touch me!"

But it was too late ... she had already placed

a comforting hand on his shoulder.

Zoe turned to cold, hard metal.

With a howl, Midas fell to his knees and wept.

"My beautiful daughter," he sobbed.

"What have I done?"

Midas clasped his hands together and prayed to Dionysus. "You were right," he said. "It was a foolish wish, and I have been such a fool. My wish wasn't a blessing, it was a curse. I beg you to take this curse from me and give me back my beautiful daughter."

Dionysus heard Midas's prayer and took pity on him. "Go to the river Pactolus," said the voice of Dionysus in Midas's head. "Wash yourself in its waters."

Midas did as he was told. He waded into the river and let the currents flow around him. He could feel his power washing away in the cool water. It seemed as though gold was pouring from his fingers, and he saw the yellow sands of the river turning to gold.

Midas felt weary when he returned to the palace. But then he saw that his gardens were no longer golden, and he could smell the scent of roses again. He ran into the palace and found his daughter waiting for him. "My beautiful Zoe," he cried. "I thought I'd lost you."

Midas called his servants and gave them each a share of his gold. "Keep some for yourselves," he said. "And the rest, give to the poorest people in my kingdom."

"But Father," said Zoe. "You love gold."

Midas shook his head. "I've learnt my lesson,"

he said. "I have been greedy and foolish. After all ...

what good is gold when you cannot eat or drink?

And what good is gold when you have

no one to love?"

Things to think about

1. Why do you think Zoe smiles "sadly" at the beginning of the story?
2. Why do you think that Midas does not listen to Dionysus when the god does not want to grant the wish?
3. King Midas's wish brings unhappiness not just for him, but for his servants and family. Do you think this is fair?
4. When does King Midas realise that his wish is not a gift but a curse?
5. Do you think that King Midas feels happier at the beginning or end of the story? What has he learned?

Write it yourself

One of the themes in this story is greed. Now try to write your own story with a similar theme.

Plan your story before you begin to write it.

Start off with a story map:

• a beginning to introduce the characters and where and when your story is set (the setting);

• a problem which the main characters will need to fix in the story;

• an ending where the problems are resolved.

Get writing! Try to use lots of superlative adjectives (for example, richest, tasiest, finest) to demonstrate your characters' greed.

Notes for parents and carers

Independent reading
The aim of independent reading is to read this book with ease. This series is designed to provide an opportunity for your child to read for pleasure and enjoyment. These notes are written for you to help your child make the most of this book.

About the book
This version of the Greek myth tells the story of King Midas, his wish to be able to turn everything he touches into gold, and the misery that this greedy wish brings him.

Before reading
Ask your child why they have selected this book. Look at the title and blurb together. What do they think it will be about? Do they think they will like it?

During reading
Encourage your child to read independently. If they get stuck on a longer word, remind them that they can find syllable chunks that can be sounded out from left to right. They can also read on in the sentence and think about what would make sense.

After reading
Support comprehension by talking about the story. What happened?
Then help your child think about the messages in the book that go beyond the story, using the questions on the page opposite. Give your child a chance to respond to the story, asking:
Did you enjoy the story and why? Who was your favourite character?
What was your favourite part? What did you expect to happen at the end?

Franklin Watts
First published in Great Britain in 2019
by The Watts Publishing Group

Copyright © The Watts Publishing Group 2019

Series Editors: Jackie Hamley and Melanie Palmer
Series Advisors: Dr Sue Bodman and Glen Franklin
Series Designer: Peter Scoulding

A CIP catalogue record for this book is
available from the British Library.

ISBN 978 1 4451 6511 0 (hbk)
ISBN 978 1 4451 6512 7 (pbk)
ISBN 978 1 4451 6841 8 (library ebook)

Printed in China

Franklin Watts
An imprint of
Hachette Children's Group
Part of The Watts Publishing Group
Carmelite House
50 Victoria Embankment
London EC4Y 0DZ

An Hachette UK Company
www.hachette.co.uk

www.franklinwatts.co.uk